What have you done to our ears to make us hear echoes?

What have you done to our ears to make us hear echoes?

poems

Arlene Kim

milkweed
editions

Published 2011 by Milkweed Editions
Printed in the United States
Cover design and art by Michelle J. Kim
Interior design by BookMobile Design and Publishing Services
The text of this book is set in Adobe Garamond Pro
11 12 13 14 15   5 4 3 2 1
First Edition

Please turn to the back of this book for a list of the sustaining funders of Milkweed
Editions.

Library of Congress Cataloging-in-Publication Data

Kim, Arlene.
    What have you done to our ears to make us hear echoes? : poems /
Arlene Kim. — 1st ed.
        p.   cm.
    ISBN 978-1-57131-440-6 (alk. paper : acid-free paper)
    I. Title.
    PS3611.I4529W47 2011
    811'.6—dc22

                                                                2011012992

This book is printed on acid-free paper.

for LB

Contents

What have you done to our ears to make us hear echoes?

"Now wake up it's time to eat! Show me
your tongue, my sweet ...

Boil her down to bone."

Rot

Begin

An apple. Experts agree that it starts with an apple.

*

Rot

* *

Lesson

For beginning metaphysicists and people of color

A person walks into a room. In this particular story, there is a table in the middle of the room. A tempting red apple sits on the table. The person sees red, sees just the skin of apple—not the flesh, or the seeds, or the table, or even the room. And certainly not the story. Not yet. The apple is of color. The person is of color. The apple has the property of redness. The person has the property of color. Apples can have redness, but redness can't have apples. And people—people can have color (and apples and stories), but mostly color *has* people.

Rot

* * *

The Seed

It's evening in the 1700s.   Korea (Mother tells me). Palace girls gather in their nightclothes and pass peaches.   Something's too sweet, soft. Someone strokes the peach hair—small, blushing head. It shimmers. The fuzz makes her stomach turn. Sometimes she craves, sometimes she sickens. Tonight, she craves. (The secret is this: the peaches are wild with worms. The secret is this: suck rot for beauty.)   Such girlish secrets worms plunder from every aging heart. Pray tomorrow she's not pocked with years like a pit. Fatten pretty on each fleshy grub; thieve from the graveyard's hearty worker. Harder to see than swallow, she blows the candles out   *whhhhhhhhhh*   the sound, too soft, sweet. She sickens, swallows.

Rot

* * * *

Never, Never

The apple is red. R e d d e n i n g . The peaches are ripe.
R i p e n i n g . They progress—imperfect; ongoing; they do not rot.
T h e y d o n o t e v e r r o t .

Spindle

I am a nickel of girlhood gone,
spun feverfew once in my pouch
with foxtail and thistledown robbed from the finches. And you

stood with me too, gathering the world then, our song
collective. We were sister thieves. We were
a siege of bitterns, a deceit of lapwings, a quarrel, a filth,
a choir of things unspanieled,
hatless, wolfless, found—

a cobbler's half mold, a comb with no teeth
by a frame with no glass, a hatmaker's block
wound with braids part-straw-and-gold,
in a field of pasque flowers nodding like chins
the cloak of a bear and a bucket on a long broken chain.

Kept in mama's sweet box, rudely stamped with trace,
scrup scrup we scraped the grounds
for every alias from the archipelago
of the missing.

Who we were
is unimportant—
that we are
come to undo.

One of Us

*. . . nine skeletons were exhumed from a shallow mass grave . . . where were the
bones of the two younger . . . ?*
    —*Robert K. Massie,* The Romanovs

*When the axe came into the woods, the trees whispered to one another, "The
handle is one of us."*
    —*Turkish proverb*

> Your name, I will tell you—
>   first there was Rasputin,
>   stumbling pilgrim. Brother,
>   crouched small in the bath, clutching
>   Mother
>   on mornings the army knelt iron-heavy
> to the tsar. How do these weigh
>   with the grease of sewing
>   machines,
>   sweat of stale skin trapping
> the bone-smooth of you?

> Let the shroud fray a river, an inked ribbon;
> polish the handle of your heart each day; restart
> to the blunt rhythm of rebirth, reworked.   Rewind.

> Remember your face in the gilt mirrors,
> the portrait, the scars. Unseat
>   the glass wings nested
>   in the egg's hollow heart. Sever the thread,
>   the braid of labor. Loose
>   the bobbins from the cruel spindles,

strew them on the current
                    like apples.
      Pass through every eye, then choose

      your name. Your fortune
reversed, hew what holds you
to that grave's dirty hem. Ravel

into the lap of woods. Roots
                    trace many stories;
            branches cradle secrets; birds,
                                on the other hand,

                        do not trust
                                    birds.

The Scar

We were poor. We were many
things. Unsaid: "good
with an axe" was one. Not always.
That was a time of war in the woods,
when all the Mothers left. We waited
for others to come. We made our own
from straw and barley. Aprons
from azaleas, sweetgrass. Father, gone,
too, in the woods, always
the woods.

That was after Sister had been stolen,
had come back missing
some small part. ("Tigers"
she said.) She knew new things, too,
like the safety of green
and how to bind your belly
with rope when hungry.
Also, how to tend wounds. Hers
like a rough braid, puckered,
an interruption of her she rubbed
when she washed, when she thought

I wasn't looking. For Father
we had Sharp Axe, for Mother,
Elder Besom. Felled, so many. Sister,

empty yourself into sleep. Your bitten pieces
will never grow back. If you keep still now,
I will close
myself in too,
into the small spaces
to weave for you
from sedge
more sister.

Bird Call

We lay there, nodding, playing the old game.
  Thrush, I said, eyes opened against sleep.
    Hummingbird, hers.

      Mother named us after birds—
          Dove, Starling, Sparrow, Wren—
        to keep together. "Her little chicks." She called;
we called back.
We were young;
we chased each other under
          her skirt. And when we grew,
              we grew together.
              We sat in the branches

                  (kneecaps touching)

      and tried to name
as many birds as barbules on a fallen feather's vane.
              Letters touching.

      Dodo sewn to hummingbird.
        Ostrich, born half-osprey. Then my
            plummeting
        Hawk, chasing her
        Kiwi. There were

        so many in the way—each leaf a
                wayward face. Every name
    pricked me

                    evergreen.

                              I thought,
"i i i i i,"

                    I saw   the slim needle of a beak
                                        opening to receive
                        a worm,
                        a crumb.

No
   one called
            back.
Lost, I had no answer. Nest
            unsafed, left
                 elopement the only way.

                         Ibis, she tossed me, re-knotting name
                              to name. We lay there.
                                        The old game.

Rib

& when we lie down again, I curl around this rib, my own, to poke at the strings of myself, hear how I've been. So much can be done with one bald rib. Dig, swat, scratch, smooth the soil under which I have buried the sound of everything that follows us.

(Were we to run from here to there—then turn—would we recognize the way back? Our path in reverse?)

We quit, we quit. Such a collage of leaving. The virtue of the runaway is all that closing of eyes between the first door, the next. We prefer wilderness to gardens. In that dark, we take shape.

Even if we fall, if they chew us to dust, my rib will burrow in a secret pocket of earth, wait there in that knuckle of silence until it is safe to make sound again, to start again. Undone, it returns to the soil where beetles dig for it a deeper bed. Fire ants nibble into it a syllabary with a hundred sounds for homecoming. Worms mate with it; a myna unearths it again. Night nourishes it with quiet until it is ready to be reborn into the throat of the next world for something like singing—

& yes—for just a foolish bit of beauty.

"Mother, look what I have brought . . .

My jug all in bits."

Needle

When she left, she left home, left all behind but her children,
    husband, and the sewing-
machine. "This," she thought, "can keep us together until it is done."
    And by this, she
meant

    the dip of the sharp eye and tip   walking
        the hem, piecing torn   parts;   by
            this, she meant the ripping of land, seam by seam,
          orphaned

                        threads splayed.   All
she took, she hoisted on her back

    one way or another; the machine
    she held on her head. She tread
    road, just barely at times, the pace
                ongoing, like
                    muslin through the feed-
                    dogs. Outrun

the seam ripper. Her
husband the presser foot; her girls, small
        bobbins. What was
            left   for her
            but to   be-
                              come
                        the
                            needle.

A country is sewn in squares. Land reveals our stitching, our appetite for peopling in four-sided polygons, in right angles, nearly. But then the forest. What doesn't sit straight, pace neat in known lines. Even when she has nothing, she saves

        scraps,   practices passing

                         thread

       through the eyes   of her girls—

                old patterns   to keep

                              sharp.

Reasons We Left

Her side was where we walked till we burned
in smoke. This is what flesh becomes:
a warning. A charred aspen.

In a storm, an axe tied to a branch
makes a hollow call. Old horse trickery.

Morning comes like a slap. The idiot sun idling
unconcerned over each crocus
chewed by plague, by footpath.

It's no time to be sweet—we are tender,
flammable, so light, we are the orphaned ones of lovers.

> I heard the bugle. Pressed drops of emergency
> to my eardrums, dried them to my cochlea.
> Mane of music—never not amazing.

Soon evening smells of apples, the world
rises like bread. We wait to harvest
what grows, but we are not the only ones.

Many hungry mice scrabble at night
in the patterns of the young, meandering,
as we do these days, thought-to-thought, uninformed
but surrounded by facts, leaving now and then
a tallowy trail.

We left because we were lost and broken.

       Because our dough faces and bloomblack hair displeased you.

       Because we had but a dried heel of apricot remaining among us.

       Because the way was lit only by hard stones.

       Because we found the false axe and did not want to go back.

Answers to the Proust Questionnaire

Coldly the wind fell upon them
In many majesties of sound
——Wallace Stevens

Q. Your most marked characteristic? What is it
　　you most dislike?　　　What faults
　　do you most indulge?　　What
　　do you most admire
　　　　　　　in a man?
　　　　　　　in a woman?

Q. Favorite virtue?
Q. Favorite name?
　　　　　Favorite
　　　　　　　　　bird?

Q. The greatest of misfortunes? Q. Principal defect?
　　　　　Q. Present state of mind? Q. Lowest depth of misery?

A. *fear:* a dark blue fly—fell
milk-fried, de-buzzed, mummi-
fied, sanitized, swatted, twitching, octo-
pi'd, then occupied, then

parched in paper, baked in pie,
a piper's lie, beauty unpied,
beauty unpied, beauty　unpied beauty unpied
standardized, pig-sty'd, pigeon-shyed, wing tied
& tied & tied to Mother's tide, dragged
　　along a gutter's side, tongue-bitten ride, all time to bide,

curbed & cowed, deered, moused, nailed,
tax -onomied -dermied, dummied, ginger-stuffed & stuck
in batter, stuck
in fence, lungs hung, ambered & de-

voweled, droned in Aeschylean wail, ideas loused,
buttered, bitten, spat from mouth,

from mattress, from garden, from chancel maw, toad-spew not jewels
spat   from wood from whale from veins   word-skeins

        thoughtthatflight   that sky   white-

washed,   threshed,   lexis-
                        drowned,   sunk face
                                        first, bye
                                        classic-

                                torso, legs   paled,
                                            f (ǀ) ailed,
                        in order, pinned

                t-o   l-i-n-e   t-o   d-r-y

                they that had left the flame-freaked sun

                to seek a sun of fuller fire

                what to do, what to do

Season of Frogs

Mother preferred the mountain,
though she rarely went
for fear of hawks circling
there (there was much to fear
in the world, she said), she said
she liked high places, the wind
on her puffed cheeks, the sound of crickets
singing from the river below.

Was this where we had first been born,
we who watch the river now?
What stilled you with fear, Mother?

At night we sing all our questions to the trees:
  Who widowed the mothers? Who ate up the husbands? Who
    left us
  with just this crippling cry?
    More things than hawks can steal.
  Why did you leave us, Mother? Why did you not try harder
    to sew
    the song of you
    firmly to our tongues?

I hate the river and all its sadness.
I hate the long, rainy season of regret, of wayward frogs.

There is more world
and it is too sweet
to deny. Though I tried
to listen, I could not
follow your song,

Mother, the world was too loud,
and I was a lonely child not a country.

Now that you have left me, I will leave, too,
become the world's. And the world,
though it wishes,
cannot leave me.

Hollow Tongue

The dead can speak
any language, I'd imagine,
but did those quiet years dull your tongue,
Halmuni?
How many words died
each evening you waited
for us to come home.
Silence, stale in your mouth
as you sat smoking Salems
aimlessly twisting
the ring on your finger,
while your favorites
   (Captain Kirk, Kung Fu, the Bionic Woman, her Six Million
    Dollar Man)
moved their mouths to sound.
Good, evil—easy
to understand, not like

us, except when we rose,
wordless, tongues drumming staccato notes
   (d- d- d- d-   d- d- d- d-   d-d-d-d-   dddd)
sewing rhythm and sound to the slow-motion running,
the leap over walls: absurd, bionic.
This, you understood,

like the white Jesus hung
in the room we shared, like
your life: duty in symbols, iconic
   (the war, your son, his children, this country)
hard words you moved your mouth to.

Now your tongue lies hard, cold
jade, mislaid
ring. The center,
the sound: rot hollow.

I'm Sorry, Father, for Losing the Key

Best when a storm hits fast and cruel—hard like punishment.

I should have known not to let the house key go.

How many times must Father tell me. His belt hit the meat
of my calves, drawing with each lash, a long welt, a stripe.
We are strange animals.

Don't cry, he warned. There were anthills by the cement
where I'd squatted, smeared the scent trail, interrupted the steady
                                                    collecting

of crumb, of soil. Then sweet air. Thunder. Dark, distant.
I saw in the yard the new dogwood, how it swayed, trembling
in anticipation. Each raindrop, a thrill; every torn petal, cheated
                                                    bittersweet.
How many wonders there were in one afternoon.

Though each strike cut deep, I couldn't stop
remembering. Was it wrong?
I held tears tight, as he said I must, while my colt legs
bowed. For all the mislaid keys,
I paid. I paid to buy this trick of conjuring
a panic of ants, the path come apart, sweat shining
on my father's brow, the milk of summer
dogwood, and hard rain.

Spool, Book, Coin

1. (A child
enters
a dark wood,
path lost
from the start.)

Her womb
split open
bore us
from old blood.
One child

at a time,
she taught
how the world
cut names
in us all.

For nine
cloistered months,
Mother
was the world
I ate.

From her tongue
I grew
and fattened.
to girl,
to daughter.

The way
thick with toads,
tigers,
woodcutters
and deer—

familiar
to some,
nonetheless
our own.
One year passes.

Listen.
They call me

"2." Now
I must tell
our tale:

how histories
repeat
in a maze,
how they
won't let go

our hands,
so afraid
we'll lose
direction
or start

a new track,
running
from our first
stories
like rabbits

hunted
by wild dogs
who snuff
us out. *Hush,*
Sister!
> *Be chary*

of each
step. Mother
waits. She
devises

3 paths:
spool, book, coin.

She lets
us go. We
leap hell-
bent, broken,
starved.

What could
each path hold?
Long days,
life in words,
fortune.

Mouth, hands
reaching.
I hear time
    pulsing—
       fickle,
quicksilver.

Choose.

Verna

And where is Verna? . . .
Light years away, by your measurements.
. . . A little hard to get to, then, wouldn't it be?
　　—*Jack Finney,* Of Missing Persons

It was the first word I learned
　　for paradise, beyond. There
　　　　would be more words, soon,
but then, there was *Verna.*
　　The textbook didn't give the date (1955) or call it
　　　　science fiction. No matter.
　　　　　　Mother worked in a bank; Father courted escape; they
　　　　　　　　both settled
　　　　　　　　　　down for life. And missing persons—
　　　　I had many names for those already.
So Finney's "Charley" I met like family.

Over years, I'd lost the author's name,
　　forgotten titles, people, exact circumstances. But not the barn,
　　　　not the tiny drifts of damp confetti on the floor—tickets
　　　　　　punched in a pattern of tiny holes,
not Charley, alone in the dark, the rain,
　　wishing he'd stayed, believed the way
　　　　you must if you've left
　　　　　　Egypt behind for Canaan.

What promise the 50s held, drew
　　back,—I don't know—nor what struggle
　　　　Finney faced, from what he ran. The night
　　　　　　the North took mother's father, marched him

into the dark, there might have been rain, confetti.
That date, too, gone, long since;
like Charley, he returned, voided,
    pricked in a pattern of tiny holes.

Parallels get drawn in bewildering designs,
    for order, for purpose. We trust.
        I try to know better, to know history
            from fiction, science from sanctity, yet,

            what to believe when one night, alone
                at the bus stop, I see the stubs of our faith
                    skitter about me? How long to pause
                before opening the barn door?

Once, I Held Time

Daughter, a lie I told & here the lie untell. In my palmed half-shells I
                                                                    held
for you a magic I made, some devilry. Easy then to bend
a fact, a thing into a brightly conjured charm, tick-ticking in collusion.
"Look what I've caught"—there was Time, confined.
There, in my hand, a fragile breathing, its pulse beat seconds, mean
                                                                    & thin.
You peered at the needle heart. "& those? the frozen
arms?" "They move; they will." Like witching rods searching,
tracking, jerking to. Years, nothing to you yet, no—not
a device, you saw, but all the world's minutes, stayed. You pleaded,
"Let me." I let you cradle the beast I said I'd glassed.
"& this crack?" Unlucky flaw. "Yes, that splintered place. It tried once
                                                                    to run
but fell as it fled, cried out when it fractured. I recaptured
the traitor, but left it unmended. Its punishment, this unsteady psalm."
We listened to the broken sound, then I bound it
firmly by its strap, before it tore free. Once, I held Time, not it me.

Exhibit A: Archive

This piece lent by Jong-Jin Kim and Soon-Sup Soh

In Korea, a girl with a single long braid meant something (unwed).
Here it means something else (native).
To mother, Korean and now here, it means foreign (unwanted).

Primary collection: Grandmother, her son, his daughters.
Secondary collection: Mother, her daughters.
Tertiary collection: Daughters (sisters).

Mother lent us her hair for exhibit. It grew the same on us,
her clutch, her collection. Oh, we must not cut it,
the rope to her, the inherited line.
But that was an ancient time. She says
we must now forget it, untie ourselves. Only knots remain—she
ties and unties them every evening.

In the photograph
    Untitled, 198—
see how we borrow her,
how we lean with no direction
against each other
like the tulips that background us.
Hair: cut rough, tips flay out, untethered.
On our stems: reversed calyxes.

Our hair is black; the tulips, red & yellow; our clothes, red & yellow
                          & black & white &
                                      blue.

We twin; we sway between knots; we try to catch the pollen
                              falling from our overturned
                                                    cups.

which way (spool)
which way (book)
which way (coin)

     —mother does not remember what we chose   —we sift the pollen

—which (spool) which (book) which (coin)   —she says she does not
                              remember which which which

                                   ( )   ( )   ( )

          —this partial cutting, imperfect collection

"There is bad in the wood

(this is where children get lost
for good)..."

Wilderness

The wind is the true breath; the horizon, the best line.
        Oh, god, how did we get here?
Let us in to where you make things,
into the clearing. We are trying, but it is hard to coax our way
from the yeasty mouth of the thicket,
this embarrassment of crusts.

We find a trail:

wort :: word
wald :: wood
weld :: world
wunde :: wound
warte :: wait

We listen and wait

        to grow wild again.
       We see the field
           is not in the word,
           it is in the world.

         We walk deeper
            into the paint of night.

Translation Plundered

after Anna Akhmatova,
after Stanley Kunitz & Max Hayward,
after Judith Hemschemeyer

Everything is plundered, chanced again, comrade, traitor, fence.
Gone, the feathers, plucked and traded; we had to—
with just thin broth for our hunger—they owed us,
but we learned their songs, didn't we,

before every bird disappeared from the woods. The woods
that eat children, like cherries. Little children, jam cherries. Run.
At night, the Seven Sisters shine like bones, seeking,
but nothing is clear—especially not here, in the dear wood.

We sleep unbathed in groves, beneath the sky bankrupt with storms.
It fills with dirty stars hunting for the lost chestnut, the oiled fable of us.
We hide ourselves again and again in the tangle, scavenging, lifting
                                        our own weight,
                    measuring our flesh day to day, to give to the night,
to the woods, which has promised to feed us from its babbled breast,
                                                    for now.

Tiger-Brother

Letter: Antonin Dvořák to his children
Otilka, you are the oldest and most sensible and I depend on you . . .
Be good then . . . remember what I say . . .

Letter: Antonin Dvořák to Anton Seidl
. . . And now the horrible story between mother and witch is going on . . .

Mother passed to me
her tiger, cruel and hungry, come
to make of me his meal if I went on
disobeying. Beast
left wandering, left guarding what
forms he could not become. Im-
patient himself, he could not wait 100 days
to see the sun. He left the Bear to his own
story. It's always this way, it seems, two
brothers, parting—the good and bad
one—creating nations
of believers, of sinners. Tiger-Brother

prowls now, keeps watch on all
the young from mother's line,
hunts what he lost, ready to take you
from home, your true fear.
Drag you like meat
to an unknown lair, where
soon you, too, will go
unknown. Home, you imagine,
goes on forgetting you. Dear

naughty children, there is no negotiating, no
escape by riddle.
There is just being
swept off under a warm, coarse coat.
No more family, no more
name. Lost in strange music,
it is hard to tell, mother
or tiger? Both

hold you close
to their breast, their line. *Don't
forget,* a ghost rumor, a breath
like a door opening, closing—
It's hard to tell which. I have

never seen a guardian angel.
Though tigers are plenty. And grim
tales. All the ways of lapsing.
I have forgotten, Mother. I pass
unschooled, unchurched. I wander in the wood,
thimbles spent, pecked by evening's thousand beaks,
always about to meet an old woman
who will catch me
in the crook of her wizened arm, croon
foul familiar songs, stitch me
to her belly, boil away
my name, marry me to her
twig broom, her
lonely Tiger-Brother.

Release, Catch

Many lovers sought her, but she spurned them all, ranging the woods . . . Her father often said to her, "Daughter, you owe me a son-in-law; you owe me grandchildren."
      —*from* Bulfinch's Mythology

Hair slicked back like an animal's
        Daphne goes riding.
Her whip warns wild things to run
        though her girl song calls like purring.

Her father propped in hip boots
        wades for a day's catch
in borrowed waters. He waits. Patience his role
        his hand on the reel.
She rides deeper into private property uncategorized
        wildlife chasing the crack of her whip.

Her salt skin and artless tread betray
        huntress as daughter   lure
Delphi's groundsman with his dogs. He swears
        love then wedlocked bliss with verse
fed on nursery song. Daphne is bound
        to refuse the trade of whip for ring, wood for cradle.

At bay   she must run
        but her   friendless   dress
catches   slows.   Her
        hair now   loosed
knots tamed fingers   in the   strung leaves
        in the brambles   hangs her
like bait

on her father's line—
a fine catch he wrestles from river
to forest bed,
beneath the lush and many laurels.

What Lies in the Rest of the Wood

Trees do not exist as we used to know them, Sister. It's OK. We can still find a way to think of home. Look, the leaves will show us.

ᙍ

The leaves, bronzy and full of song holes, show us who has passed before. (Animals have also learned this.) A deer wearing his jacket of autumn whistles as he peers at us, then hurries off. He wears no pants. And look, there is also a hare. The danger has pierced her long twigged ears, and now, everything grows horns.

ᙍ

Everything here grows horns—and also gold. Trees get greedy, but their avarice is, at least, pretty, like a daffodil dipped in itself, over and over until it becomes only its gold light, its plate of beauty. Sleep now, Sister. It will take a long time to bloom again, and by then we will know what lies in the rest of the wood.

ᙍ

What lies in the rest of the wood? A camp of teeth. For the children of woodcutters, sweet moil. This is the scary part, Brother, the part where we thieve treasure by following the inward maps. Keep sending them your notes, your small pebbles. One day, they will let us in.

CR

They will let us in when we have found a way to marry the petrel to the man, to curve the bull's ear to our liking. His warm snout in your palm will be the sign, Brother. But do not touch the white fox. She's trapped in a noose of gold. She cannot hear you anymore—all of her color fed to the greedy trees.

CR

The greedy trees—I know, you never believed any of this, dear one, though you tried, especially when the fires died. How lucky I have made all this up—a feast of lies, Sister, to keep us from ourselves. Cover your face and the flies can't get inside you. (But remember to let me in when I ask.) The truth is we are the trees now. Remember when we slept in trees, the pines, our bed? We branch ourselves, deep in the sedimentary drop. Stay away from your favorites or you'll tangle them up in us. Pinch their gold, but leave them skinned with light. Flood your eyes with seeds. Don't look for the path back. We are the only path.

Before the Fires

Of flame we were told
to say nothing.

Don't speak to us
of wicks and matches.

All is shadowed now,
burned, blackened in the choke of ways.

Mother wouldn't like it,
but I'll tell you:

All our uncles died in fire.
Their wax bones made our family tree

fragile in the summer. So much fury
happens in the hot, hot months.

Our patterns follow the wind.
Eaves we have razed,

sucked to cinders, and the fallen
eaten up. More, we cannot say.

Too full our bellies—full of murder
and nothing.

Rabbit Song

I stood too near the warren
and when I stumbled back, the rabbits stamped in alarm.

Iambic admonition, cautionary song.

Of what in the wood did they warn? Of whom?

Tracking

Tortoises retreat
to burrow for much
of the year to avoid predators,
extreme heat.
Tucked in shells
(the shells like helmets)
they tilt heads upward
as if waiting, listening for
something. They hold
their blank chins high.
Their mouths slit with dark,
They blink, dumbed monks.
No prayer, nothing left to give away
but a box of saints.
Not one coin glints
from the maw.

Brother, let us rest here until the sun sits back down.
I will weave you a mask, whiskered and princely.

>   The first time a mask is broken: spotting. (sex)
>   The second time a mask is broken: no tell-tale stains. (hush)
>   The third time a mask is broken: there is just the mask. ( )

Something broken floats among the reeds, rotting there
among the roots of drunken trees. We are alone here with no wishes.
This is no dream, so there are no wishes. Doctors tell us
that dreams   that dreams   fulfill wishes.
But nightmares do not. Nightmares repeat trauma.

Taken to the woods again? The path, wet with the moon again?
It wasn't the ax, it was a branch he'd fastened to a dead tree
so that the wind would blow it back and forth repeating
the story of the trees. Song lost in the wind again?

Brother, let us lie a little longer. There is still some fire left, a little cake.
The sun, climbing hill after hill, falling from hill to hill, is not
dreaming.

Stalemate.
The toad
on one side of the hill,
the cricket
on the other. No one moves.
The toad is listening hard;
he does not blink;
he hears prey. The cricket

waits, legs tight.
The cricket prays
its song. Careful.
The toad is unspooling his tongue.
Now, rabbit song.

> Break after a noun: a low degree of enjambment. (sex)
> Break after an adjective or verb: a medium degree of
> enjambment.(sex)
> Break after a preposition: a high degree of enjambment. (the
> morning after)

Leaving home is the only way, Brother.
I have untied the axe from the branch.

The Squirrel

And so it was that a young squirrel traveled with her family to a rough and violent area of Virginia with their most precious family heirloom—a tin can telephone that the young squirrel's Aunt Incha had saved from being crushed by the traffic on the 99. So attracted was she to the shine, that she risked her life for this can and the trapped echoes within, polished to a brightness by the ethereal rubbing with the world. But the squirrel family soon discovered that they were not bringing hope to immigrant Virginia, but greed. Paradise became a seditious yard. The shine grew coarse and dirty; the can shouted vulgarities. The tin lost its luster, its quiet thrum; it became a black blade striped with blood. One night, the young squirrel took it and left her family, taking the dark echoes with her.

When Thunder, Then What

Running across that open field, I jammed fingers in my ears, my eyes
a kid squint. All that light in one blink, that white white light. Was
it like dying? I worried the coins I clutched in my hand would call
the lightning down like Charon's ferry. How naked I was in that pool
of grass. Every tree threatened my name. I wondered what it would
be like, to be struck with all that Frankensteinian force, those heated
amperes. A morsel forked by electricity. If in that moment before, my
brain would catch fire, flame with memories, beading, bolting—and
what of my heart? What name would be found there singed into my
light-stamped veins—Just before—would I illuminate, beam & sing
like a fragile coil of filament—throat strings caught in glass?

"Did you hear that? They answered:

There. . . . Voices . . .

It is the wind, the child of the sky."

Wind

The wind, she found me again this morning, while I was walking home. She rushed over me, frisked and sifted through me with her pickpocket habits. She was searching for something she'd left, misplaced, some sign of something she'd forgotten, thrown away in error. The small birds played in her fingers. She held the city; she held my face.

———————

Wind

Somewhere a mother is worrying her hands together. The wind runs over her fingers, trying to learn this shape, this tying hand to hand, this not letting go. She finds a similar shape in lovers.

———————

The wind is harassing me. At night,
she fights the sky, forever searching.
I tell her she won't find it, that there
is nothing there, but she doesn't
listen. She strikes me, beating my
face, exhausting my face, learning
and erasing and punishing my face
for being there, pressed against her.

———————

The wind—how fiercely she gropes me with her desperate hands, wanting
to remember and not knowing how. The way she tries to hold me
in the small, forgettable ruin of her heart. The fierceness that is her heart.
Her way of knowing the world and herself in it is to blow against all who
hold her, the mountains, the buildings. She hisses down the streets we trap
her in, wrecks the face of the frozen lake. The blind and angry wind.
Somewhere a bag of trash has ripped open; a city has ripped open; she
picks through it;
she's looking again. She always comes back,
she cannot tame herself, she cannot
know how savagely she embraces us.

———————

Wind

I stood and let her rake me as she wanted, with her scour, her gruff.
I stood and let her have that much of me. How she leaned into me
then. I brought for her a fist of grass, a wand of squirrel's tail, a
newspaper soiled with the street, knobbled twigs, joints of fence and
feather. We like to make ourselves known—the scraps of us, the trash
of us. Don't let go these pieces. We are not yet sure what they are for.

———————

Wind

Against what do we rush?

The loneliness, dumb despair.
_____

Wind

I must not forget to look into every person's face, I must not forget to do that, to search, even quietly, for gratitude, for the ones who save for me a mouthful of hope? who recall my good.

_____

Lift my face to the sting. _____

Wind

The wind, she slaps me over and over.
_____
_____

Paper Suns

My love. I tended him
after he fell. His charred wing stumps,
his elegy of scabbed feathers. Only then
would he accept a bed, me
in it. The memory burnt into his limbs
burned me, too, so that only my negative remained
in what amputated dreams he had, what
eerie ornithology haunted him. My hybrid,
neither bird nor angel—I came
to gather what boy there was left
to salvage.

I fold him paper suns, light them
on fire, hurl them skyward,
a revenge I can offer.
For a moment, the sun in his face,
twinned in his eyes.
For a moment, not the sun, but his face,
its reflection like the sun,
like an old story. In the water,
another sky, a ghost sun.
He didn't know at first
if he was falling or flying.
Which was his sun?
He, my sun.

When he fell, he splintered
and I was born.
From then I carried him.
He still burns when he sleeps—
I can scarcely touch him. Every night

I singe a part of myself, lose myself
to ash. I rock him
back to dream, and in
him, his father. We three fall
and fall toward
the salt womb, sea-bed.
F a c e s   s u n w a r d.

Turtle-Sister

Dioramas, second floor, Bell Museum of Natural History

1.
Cruel, the Creator. Whimbrel,
Herring Gull, Hudsonian God-
wit, Black-Bellied Plover—even
the Least Sandpiper all feathered,
temporary to river, to land. I am
the only non-winged thing
in this scene. Like so many visitors
to the seashore, they flock and wade,
preen and flirt with the lace of tide
washing and unwashing
over their long, slender legs.

The air swells with the white-rumped
flutter of their gabbled comings
and goings. Loudly oblivious
to the shell-grit of my days below,
one transient Tern, happy
as only a Caspian Tern can be,
whoops out to his fraternity
of masked goons. *Jerk.*

2.
I spend my days here silent, craning
toward the sky, studying flight patterns.
Thing is, if I turn my flipper just so,
it resembles a wing of sorts—though

no plumes. I am as naked and stony
as a polished pit. But I'm no feather brain.

I know about Darwin and the Galapagos.
The next turn may be mine. You've heard
of the hare—and that tortoise, she was
my sister. I think in slow and steady designs.
I've seen the smooth silver of something in the sky,
like the underside of a pearled shell. Sister,

wait for me. My thoughts race.

Litany for Common Horses

(a fallen sonnet)

Haru-urara ("glorious spring" in Japanese) loses her 106th straight race.
  —from the Associated Press

Ordinarily, you couldn't lose that many if you wanted to.
  —comment by fan Ryosuke Koshimizu

Not as easy as it looks, holding
back, timing these missteps to mimic
nature's fall from grace. This betrayal
of sinew and stride must continue
for another spring to have its place
once more after winter's brittle breath.
(Give me your tired, hungry, and poor.)
Hurry. Hurry. No savior's donkey,
like you, I do the work of father's
father, fight lost brothers, name hope, race
death. As I circle, circle apace,
an echo passing farther, fainter
through the crowd (petals plucked from night's bough),
heave your pack again, speed the circuit,

         call up the fallen, practice name by name the letting go.

No Gondolier

All born to some duty, some purpose, we practice ourselves day in,
                                                                  day-through-
                                             night. I see your gondolier

must practice, too. Of course. How else to gain the smooth and
                                             practiced hand of one who
                                             travels between worlds? To learn

the art of ferrying 'cross the Styx, holding the frail arms of the unwilling
                                                                  with one hand,
                                             with the other, swiftly plucking

the coins from their mouths, eyes, before the bright pieces plunk into
                                                                  the deeps,
                                             unrecoverable. All the while,
                                             the boat, steady.

Death, you devil, hiding your men in plain sight. A true stroke
                                             of genius, of mockery.
                                             The lean, black boat
                                             among the canoes;

his slow oaring past the paddlers, the shirt of stripes, the jaunty
                                             ribboned hat—funny—
                                             still with your divine comedy,

I see, in the way you tell your man to leave the boat at night, bobbing
                                                                  with the others,
                                             a familiar shade, unmoored,
                                             a slim, black slipper.

Echo

after Celan

out of the belly of hell cried I
 —*Jonah 2:2*

I saw how the night came.
The black milk of night

sluiced from the live port and fixed me
with its wayward stars, each
windowed glimpse an improvised constellation,
a blind map of stones.

   Passing through this living ark, I recall
   Noah and wonder how he did it,
   how he made the beasts comply,
   how he let everyone else go
   (*sinners,* he said) with one oar stroke.

   I wander the muscled decks, through piles
   of fins, occasionally strange fur. I eat
   what I can, picking meat from decay,
   drinking water thick with minnows.

When the night came—
dark bridemilk of night

shifting over the shit of life
in birth shades of brown, totem brown,
spewing more honey, more thrum
than the whitest noon,

I touched the larynx,
found a huddle of seafaring sparrows
defying their slight nature.
I spied another. Mariner, exile, émigré—
I cut from him the prisoner's heart,
packed the wound with lists of names. We spoke
of dreams and nights, of how he might invent
from ashes, living. Still

    I write their names over
    and over in a scab hue
    on the lung walls of this catacomb.
    I gather syllables, collect what earth has lost, search
    for cigarette stubs
    news of Nineveh.

When that night came—
the myth milk of night—

I suckled on the sounds of beaching,
plash of boot-steps toward shore, hum of engines
in this emptied camp, my brother's preaching, and
                      bare sparrow song.

For him: to tell, to feed, to grease, to light.
This whaled cell and I have done our part.

For me: I lapse, I lapse
    in the pitch of echoes, unlit nights.

"Sister, I think we've lost the way . . .

. . . Turn yourself around,
my slow-coach Brother"

North Was Not the Way

The lead flyer suffered from anxiety,
nightmares. He kept dreaming
they were in a dream, flying north
when north was not the way.
He tried to dream them out of it
again. (This did not work.)

Every dawn, the ground
recovered from heartbreak,
the warm winds started.
But the flock was feeling uneasy.
This felt like starting back
from where they came. But there
was so much fear in turning back.
Which direction foretold promise,
silks, a fat enough herd?
North was not the way. And back
was also not the way.

Every afternoon, he turned them around,
but they kept formation, each face
closed like a beehive, industrious.
The current welling.
It was a mistake. The dream
of migration, unclear.

The Collecting

Sister keeps collecting dead things. Bees and rag-winged dragonflies.
A frozen mouse, teeth bared like a prize. A crow, butterflied open. She
pleats them up in her apron and keeps walking. Why do they find
her at the last, the dead sparrows, the muskrats and prairie dogs, the
red squirrels, the spent tatty-sail moths. Then yesterday, a spatuletail?
It's a long way from here to Peru, she thinks, carrying him home to
snap small portraits, make a cast of wing, snug chin feathers into an
embroidery circle, bury him primly in a box of gingerbread, his strange
tail tucked so. It is the history of the forest, she says, of ways we get lost;
I would like to say how it all happened; I would like to put it right.

Among Monarchs

In the forest, the fur of Monarchs covers every tree. This is how curses
happen (or, miracles): of a sudden, unexplained. Entire populations die
during an unlucky migration. The children wander. Dried-out wings
blanket the ground like leaf-covering, woven into them the story of
some land. Flightless, they are just paper dolls. When the wind picks
up, the dead drift by on the current. Their wings, brittle; they snap as
the children submerge themselves in the endless archives. So pretty, the
veined things: probosces coiled fat, frozen antennae, thickets of needles.
The children prick their fingers on history, fall asleep to the murmuring
of multitudes. It's getting dark. Through the night, the bodies fall in
turn. Beneath the masses, it's dry, warm. The children bury themselves,
like climbing into the sun at night. Embalmed, they plot escape, pocket
handfuls of tigery gold. It was a way back once before.

Song

The Audubon Singing Bird Clock announces the time with the melodious sounds of authentic bird songs! Twelve North American backyard birds sing, each at the appointed hour. A light sensor deactivates the bird songs when the room is dark.

Does she think of her brother
when she hears a caged House Finch?
Or that house?
When a White-Throated Sparrow
trills at 10 she could be daydreaming
or drifting off to an early night,
the story in her lap, unfinished.
What does a Nuthatch sound like
at the 11th hour? Urgent warning, mother's call?
Mockingbird, Mourning Dove, Cardinal, Wren
serenade her from each perch,
all assigned a song of passing.
Time is
        a fallen feather,
        a wing beat,
        a green branch,
        a lost song,
        a coo from the rooftop,
        a fall from the nest,
        a girlish echo,
        a crimson breast,
        a breadcrumb,
        a parted beak,
        a mass migration,
        a tiny flock of seconds.

Mountains

Her daily task: to cut and conjure words
to fit the box of headlines.
Wrangling them into her bed of sizes,
she stretches and chops, loads the gun
with facts and figures, tolls and dates, places
she's never been, a thousand ways

to die. She worries she is forgetting
the little things that hold the days together.
She says as many small words as she can think of:
oh and *and,* and *not,* and *bun, fine, tot, cup, as.*
Easy words, like pebbles, like crumbs: *speck, girl, bit,*
grass, or, even *oven,* even *yarn,* even foolish words,
cheese and *chicken, smock,* even *dear,* even *love.*

Poor fugitives. They can't survive her. At night,
she tucks them up her sleeves, packs them
in a bag, in an unmarked envelope, drops them
stone by stone to find her way home
from the mountain she erects every morning
for the world to climb.

Wolf-Fruit, Rind

A tricky business with no answers. Or answers that seem like birdsong
heard by only one birder on the twitch, an elusive flutter from above.
Watching is everything in this field. I hunch over a rickety cart. Observe.
Veterans like these are likely to yield a variety of techniques worth a shot:
thumping, shaking, stroking, rolling, pinching. Even biting. I saw one.
When did a melon get this heavy, their trembling arms seem to say, the
spotted, paper skin fading among the bark of bargain cantaloupe. Their
song, more a constant twitter, sometimes a low sigh, or no song at all—
melodies lost, sung out. Men take many shapes; it's all in the watching,
the wording. Old wolf now, all muzzle and furred loping. I see what
I've come to learn: one presses a great snout close to fruit flesh and, eyes
closed, seeks some wild sweetness still lingering beneath the rind.

Curse

What do we do now
the curse has lifted?
A curse tells you
what you can and can't do
in this world. Now there is nothing
to tell the children, (how we regretted
those times dearly, dearly)
nothing to do but live our lives,
trade away the magic beans,
daughter to the foxes, our tongues
for love, even the sturdy milk cow.
We work our whole lives for a promise,
the promise of a curse
lifting—floating free from plot, from the past.
But in all that sky, we get lost.
We start to hope
we see the shape
of another curse.
We start to look for ways
to trade again.

"I learn very slowly.

Show me once more how it goes."

Occupation

We are in another country
not catching the words,
not saying what we want,
      not charioted by Bacchus and his pards,
      But on the viewless wings of Poesy we pass
      a message, slippery as silk,
from country to country, each line ripped clean
from our only common tongue, then burned
to ash, the pattern lost
      Farewell! Thou art too dear for my possessing
      And like enough thou know'st thy estimate:
      The charter of thy worth gives thee releasing
      from the cryptographer's embrace.

Is there a Navajo word for bomber?
Or does the static carry, for a charged second,
an image of a bird, wings wide,
diving, diving—

We've eaten our words before.
The taste: thin grass, boiled straw, sheet by sheet inky and metallic.
The texture: fine hairs woven tight, mesh of webs, gluey marrow.
The sound: German, Japanese, English
      Take it, and eat it up; and it shall make thy belly bitter,
      but it shall be in thy mouth sweet as honey words
      to camouflage the root.

Quantityless, nameless, we are
ciphers of this time, agents of history, our mouths
overflow with the vocabulary of the foreign,
forbidden. We survive by myth,
by numbers, by verse *to hear each other's whisper'd speech;*

Eating the Lotos day by day, we cut the mother tongue, beloved,
but cannot forget our derivation.

If our transmission is successful, trace us back
through translation, diagram the journey
of our mute longing. We repeat:

> *I cut the cold night, take its long waist to my bed,*
> *curl quiet under the seam of spring, wait.*
> *When you return for me, I will unravel.*

"the path come apart"

The principle is expressed in Latin as "the children
submerge themselves in the yard, burrow into a broken bone."

* * *

By this she meant, the ripping of her at night. She tucks the small scars
between girl and woman, with enough hair to resemble a wing of
sorts. There were high winds, temptations spanning a room, an apple
on the current.

* * *

Without flight, they grow horns and sing in their nightclothes, hair
slicked like an eye. We have been here before.

* * *

Wake up. It's evening in the egg's hollow heart. Time to gather names,
my peach-daughter.

* * *

Night sluices from the spindles, the fires. Sister, first, knead the
dumplings. Crumble hunger into the huddle of night. Now sleep,
Sister. You are the oldest, so be good. Me, I lapse, I lapse, I lapse, I
lapse. (Mother tells me.)

* * *

A person walks into a thousand black birds. When he wakes, he drinks
the night. The work of poison. Brother, let us rest here in the sun's eyes.

* * *

It seems I am always about to meet an old story: Mother in the woods, rubbing the world, lit by a stone slit with crumbs. Crumbs spilling from her mouth, preaching and dirty, the wild with the good. The rabbits' song steadily gathering, throat strings caught in morning.

* * *

We gather in the seed. Soon, soon, you are a ripe star cut from night. Marry me in the apple. Fall in a tear. Sever the sun by starving brightness. Meet me in the echo. There is all the path still left to sew.

* * *

What have you done to our ears to make us hear echoes?

Legend

seed: sister

the field: tall, tall girls

fruit: fruit

line: a light always moving through the field, the wood

slipper: marriage by capture, the brother run away

frog: half-mother, lost, unbraided in the field

birds: the shape of shame and what is about to happen

basket: a tiny comma growing a sister, a brother

the wood: inappropriate, half-spoken

Hunt, Peck

A tyro, at the keys, I start a field
with stalks, bent.
Venture in, hunting, pecking,
to see, what? —now:

chickens. Inelegant, graceless.
Beaky pullets. Pillow-
breasted, neck and caw, claw,
jab. Kernels pricked, break.
Dropped and pecked. Uneven
stabs. A nib, a nibble. Sharp pecks
per seed. Each seed a letter.
Pock. Pock.

ভ

Into the woods I walked. I went alone.
Though I was afraid, I pretended
not to be. Every falling leaf
made a sound. And every bird, landing,
lifting again. I, too. Up
ahead in the path, a doe
emerged from a copse.
I stopped. She, too.
I stared and stared as long as she let me.

The Cutting

Sister, I have saved this for you
to take on your way.
You will need it to make a path
through the trees, huddled
against you. The knives
I have taken from Mother's kitchen,
the axe from Father's sack,
and here, my skinning blade.
I know the danger, but there are times
when you must cut yourself
out from the belly of home.
Claim the blade. The cutting
is not to be feared as much
as the sowing. A seed,
a flame we fan in silent slices,
sharp wishes. What we cannot say
with words begins to smolder.
Go now before the fire
scalds your name. I have buried it
in the rice field, Sister, to feed
my memory with you
until the rains wash it far from here.
When they send the wind to spy,
hide your face in your skirts.
Take this oil to bake
chrysanthemum petals
and smooth the knives.
Turn the edges away when you bathe;
they are hungry blades, but their shine is a map.
When I go to the wood to catch rabbits,

the stones will report how you are
so build an altar with each you find.
Goodbye. Press no coins
into my palm, my heart.

Acknowledgments

Much of this work was written with the support of the MFA Program of the University of Minnesota. My thanks to them for their invaluable guidance—especially to Ray Gonzalez, Bill Reichard, Michael Dennis Browne, Maria Damon, and Julie Schumacher. And my deep gratitude to the sponsors and judges of the Department of English Fellowship for Poetry, the Marcella DeBourg Fellowship, the Gesell Award, and the Academy of American Poets James Wright Prize.

To my fellow writers—Ryo Yamaguchi, Nate Slawson, Ann Linde, Emily Bright, Marge Manwaring, Anne Overstreet, Liz Gamberg, Carol Kelly—and to the teachers I had in Seattle—Derek Sheffield, Jan Wallace, Shannon McRae, Linda Bierds—many and warm thanks for your keen and weird observations, your encouragement, your good humor and camaraderie.

Grateful acknowledgement to the editors of the literary journals that first published my work: *Switched on Gutenberg, DMQ Review, Cha, Cant, DIAGRAM,* and *Blackbird.*

Thank you to Jim Cihlar and Wayne Miller for your excellent editorial counsel. And to Milkweed for this book.

To my parents, for their strength.

Dear sister, for wandering the path with me so I wouldn't be alone.

Reader, you are here, too, keeping me company. Thank you.

And Laurion, for so much and much.

Notes

The section epigraphs are from the 1893 opera *Hänsel und Gretel,* which was a sibling collaboration: the music was written by German composer Engelbert Humperdinck; the libretto text was written by his sister, Adelheid Wette.

"One of Us" was written after reading about Anna Anderson, who claimed to be Anastasia Romanov, youngest daughter of Russian Tsar Nicholas II. Many believed that Anastasia and her brother somehow survived the execution of the royal family by the Bolsheviks.

"Answers to the Proust Questionnaire" uses a line from the poem "How to Live. What to Do" by Wallace Stevens. It was also influenced by W.H. Auden's poem "Musée des Beaux Arts" and Marcel Proust's answers to the questionnaire he made famous.

"Season of Frogs" is based on the Korean folk tale of the disobedient frog. He buries his mother in the river instead of on the mountain as she wanted, and so he stays up all night croaking in lament that her body might wash away. One version of this story can be found in the book *Korean Folk & Fairy Tales,* retold by Suzanne Crowder Han.

In "Hollow Tongue," the word *halmuni* is Korean for grandmother.

"Spool, Book, Coin" refers to a traditional Korean birthday celebration. On a child's first birthday, parents set out objects on a table and watch to see which one their child picks. The chosen object symbolizes the child's path in life: money for a wealthy future, pencils or books for academic success, a thread for longevity, etc. In the Korean system, a baby is considered one year old at the time of birth, so although the first birthday celebrates a child's first year of life in the world, the child would actually be two years old. The form of this piece—alternating two- and three-count syllabic lines—was my way of mimicking the wavering footsteps of a young child and the wavering identity between child and parents.

In "Exhibit A: Archive," the braid refers to the way Korean women used to keep their hair in a long, single braid until they married. In the Korean Confucian tradition, long, uncut hair, for both men and women, was a sign of filial piety and respect for one's ancestors: one was not to damage anything bestowed by one's parents.

"Translation Plundered" is what I call an echo translation—that is, an English-to-English "translation" of or conversation with the poem "Everything Is Plundered…" by Anna Akhmatova, as translated by Stanley Kunitz & Max Hayward, and also by Judith Hemschemeyer.

In "Tiger-Brother," the epigraphs are from letters written by the Czech composer Antonin Dvořák. In 1896, Dvořák wrote a series of symphonic poems based on Czech folk tales written as ballads by Karel Jaromir Erben. In the second epigraph, Dvořák refers to his symphonic poem The Noon Witch (Polednice), B. 196 (Op. 108).

"Tiger-Brother" also references the founding myth of Korea. According to the myth, a tiger and a bear who wanted to become human were told by the sky god to stay in a cave for 100 days. The tiger left the cave before the time was over; the bear remained and was transformed into a woman who married the sky god. Their child became Korea's first king.

"Tracking" contains a line from a version of the "Hansel and Gretel" story translated by Lore Segal in the book The Juniper Tree and Other Tales from Grimm.

"When Thunder, Then What" is for Kyung.

If the dioramas mentioned in "Turtle-Sister" are still at the University of Minnesota's Bell Museum, I recommend visiting them; they are old-fashioned and wonderful. Thanks, Julie, for taking us there.

I call "Litany for Common Horses" a fallen sonnet because I had been trying to write a good sonnet for awhile—and failing for awhile. Around that time, I came across a story about a Japanese racehorse famous and beloved for consistently failing. That suggested this form to me: a sonnet done in a syllabic count of ten, rather than in iambic pentameter, in which the last count of the fourteen lines is missing and drops to a fifteenth line that gathers up the fallen syllables.

"Echo" was written while reading a collection of Paul Celan poems, including and especially the well-known poem "Death Fugue," as translated by Michael Hamburger.

"Among Monarchs" refers to an unusual migratory event that occurred in a mountainous area of western Mexico. In January 1996, a rare snowstorm killed millions of Monarch butterflies that had migrated there from the United States and Canada.

"Occupation" contains lines from John Keats's "Ode to a Nightingale," William Shakespeare's Sonnet 87 ["Farewell! Thou art too dear for my possessing"], the Bible, Revelation 10:9; Alfred Tennyson's "Song of the Lotus-Eaters," and a sijo poem written by Hwang Chin-I, a sixteenth-century courtesan and female poet of the Korean Yi Dynasty. The works of Keats, Shakespeare, Tennyson, and the Bible were all frequently used as poem-code ciphers in World War II. These types of codes eventually proved unreliable or easily breakable. However, the Navajo language—used in the Pacific Theater for sending coded messages—was a code that was never broken.

"the path come apart" uses lines generated from a Markov text program written as a collaboration with software engineer Laurion Burchall. He wrote the code for the program, which mimics and recombines a writer's recurring patterns in a series of text; I provided the series of text from large sections of this collection.

"The Cutting" loosely references a Korean superstition that one must offer some payment—even if just a penny—when receiving a knife or any sort of bladed object as a gift. Otherwise the knife will cut the tie between gift giver and recipient, severing their relationship.

A first-generation Korean American, Arlene Kim completed a BA in literature at Brown University, and an MFA in poetry at the University of Minnesota. She has been awarded the James Wright Prize for Poetry by the Academy of American Poets, and she currently serves as an associate editor for the *DMQ Review*. Arlene Kim lives in Seattle, and this is her first collection of poems.

More Poetry from Milkweed Editions

To order books or for more information,
contact Milkweed at (800) 520-6455
or visit our Web site (www.milkweed.org).

The Nine Senses
Melissa Kwasny

Fancy Beasts
Alex Lemon

The Book of Props
Wayne Miller

Reading Novalis in Montana
Melissa Kwasny

Rooms and Their Airs
Jody Gladding

Music for Landing Planes By
Éireann Lorsung

Milkweed Editions

Founded as a nonprofit organization in 1979, Milkweed Editions is an independent publisher. Our mission is to identify, nurture and publish transformative literature, and build an engaged community around it.

Join Us

In addition to revenue generated by the sales of books we publish, Milkweed Editions depends on the generosity of institutions and individuals like you. In an increasingly consolidated and bottom-line-driven publishing world, your support allows us to select and publish books on the basis of their literary quality and transformative potential. Please visit our Web site (www.milkweed.org) or contact us at (800) 520-6455 to learn more.

Milkweed Editions, a nonprofit publisher, gratefully acknowledges sustaining support from Amazon.com; Emilie and Henry Buchwald; the Bush Foundation; the Patrick and Aimee Butler Foundation; Timothy and Tara Clark; the Dougherty Family Foundation; Friesens; the General Mills Foundation; John and Joanne Gordon; Ellen Grace; William and Jeanne Grandy; the Jerome Foundation; the Lerner Foundation; Sanders and Tasha Marvin; the McKnight Foundation; Mid-Continent Engineering; the Minnesota State Arts Board, through an appropriation by the Minnesota State Legislature and a grant from the National Endowment for the Arts; Kelly Morrison and John Willoughby; the National Endowment for the Arts; the Navarre Corporation; Ann and Doug Ness; Jörg and Angie Pierach; the Carl and Eloise Pohlad Family Foundation; the RBC Foundation USA; the Target Foundation; the Travelers Foundation; Moira and John Turner; and Edward and Jenny Wahl.

Composition by BookMobile Design and Publishing Services
Typeset in Adobe Garamond Pro
Printed on acid-free 30% post consumer waste paper
by BookMobile